CW01651961

NOBLE EXPRESSIONS

ROY NOBLE'S EXPRESSIONS OF LOVE

ILLUSTRATED BY GREN

BBC CYMRU WALES

BBC
CYMRU
WALES

Noble EXPRESSIONS

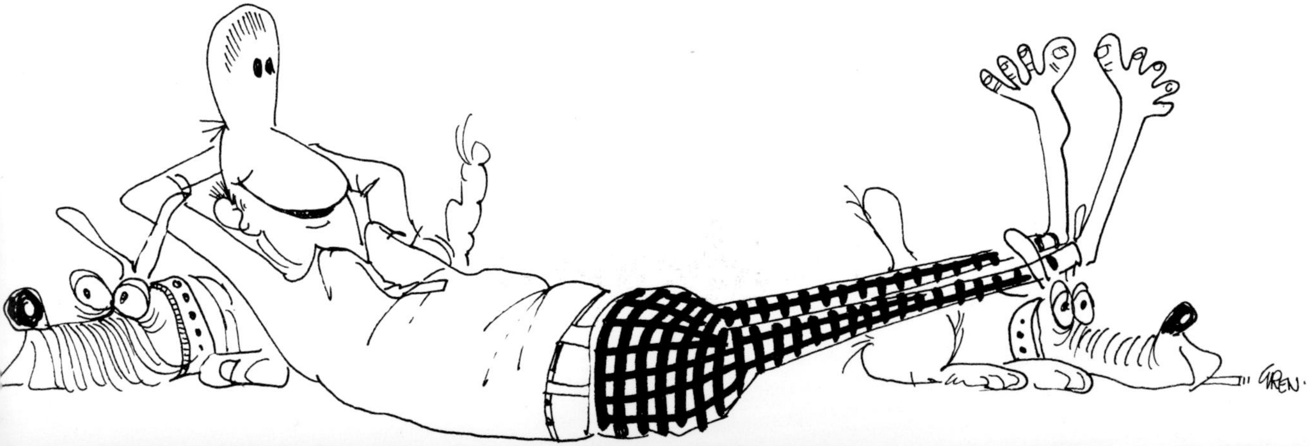

BBC
CYMRU
WALES

Published by
BBC Cymru Wales
Broadcasting House
Llandaff
Cardiff CF5 2YQ

Edited and designed by Surrexit
Typeset in Perpetua and Tekton
Cover photography by Richard Bosworth
Printed by Treforest Printing Ltd, Bedwas

© BBC Cymru Wales 1992
First published 1992

All rights reserved. No part of this work may be reproduced or transmitted by any means, electronic or mechanical, photocopying, recording, or otherwise without permission in writing from the publisher

ISBN 0 9518988 2 5

Roy Noble is one of BBC Wales' most popular and versatile radio and television presenters. Since leaving a shining career in education in 1986 his melodic tones have brought morning happiness to thousands of listeners to BBC Radio Wales.

His fervent audience following is unrivalled at the BBC studios in Cardiff, with his intimate style of presentation endearing him to thousands of followers.

Inspired by his listeners' birthday and wedding anniversary dedications over the years, Roy has composed countless romantic poems to embellish each and every message of goodwill.

With inimitable illustrations by the famed cartoonist Gren, this book brings together some of the best of those love muses heard over the airwaves.

Who knows, they may even work wonders for you!

Like laver bread and bacon,
Like sand washed by the tide,
Like mushy peas and faggots,
We belong there – side by side.

I like the way your eyes give signs –
Like signals that I've seen:
Red is stop, and amber...well,
I love it when they're green.

Ah, my love, this public face
Hides what I feel beneath;
You make me smile so wide each day
Like toothpaste on my teeth.

You're the handle on my carver;
You support me in your way;
You're the caster on my trolley
Through life's checkout every day.

In life's gamble, love, I placed a bet
And came out as a winner,
Your outpouring love makes my life complete
Just like your gravy on my dinner.

Whene'er it's cold you're there my love,
You're my heater every day;
Like the mustard on my bacon bap
You take my breath away.

In life's long test your master mind
And love will ne'er diminish;
You ask how long my love will last
Well now I've started, so I'll finish.

Like a farmer needs a tractor;
Like a postman needs a bag;
You help me with each heavy load
And you lift me when I sag.

You're the teabag to my teapot;
You're my tartar sauce on fish;
You're like jam on my rice pudding;
I'm your spoon and you're my dish.

You support me every day my love,
You're my cushion when I kneel;
You're the handle on my holdall,
You're the oil on my life's wheel.

I couldn't do without you love –
In life's boat you're my paddle;
You're my dynamo in dark filled days,
On life's bike you're my saddle.

You're the scarf that warms my winter,
In tasks you're such a toiler;
You're the butter on my cracker;
You're the wood block in my boiler.

You help me through when things are hard,
On moves you are my checker;
You help each bit on twists and turns,
You're my life's Black & Decker.

You're my answer to life's puzzle,
My solution to each quiz,
And you're bubbly and refreshing,
In life's pop you're my fizz.

Like your dishcloth to my long johns
On the line, and blowing free;
Like the flagstones to our patio set
I like you close to me.

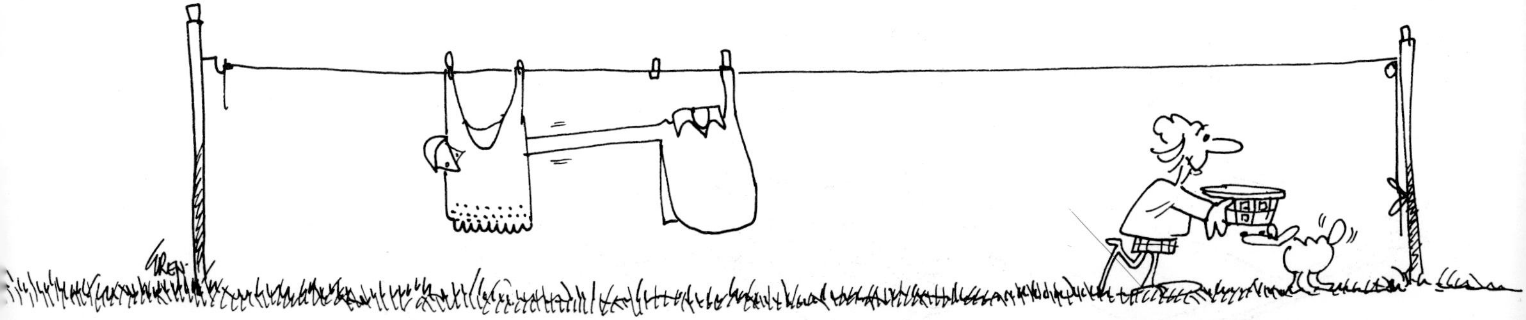

In life I feel secure –
You're the padlock on my shed;
You give me warmth and goodness,
You're the toaster to my bread.

You're the pencil to my paper,
You're the answer to my "why?",
You're the curtains to my window –
You draw me, that's no lie.

You give me strength in waking hours,
You're there whene'er I cry;
You're the 'lastic in my stocking,
You're the ointment on my sty.

You're the braces on my trousers –
Support in every way;
Like the hanky in my pocket
I need you every day.

Like the hood upon my mackintosh,
Like a fire in cold weather,
Like the grays with my blue blazer
You know we go together.

Like the perfume you wear on Fridays
You've got this way of knowing;
It's like the kick-start on my scooter –
You know what gets me going.

You're the button on my brolly,
You're the sigh in every squeeze,
You're the casters on my trolley,
You're my hanky when I sneeze.

Those stolen moments coyly shared –
Recalled as if by knack –
As the usherette cried "None of that,
Take your hand from 'neath your mac."

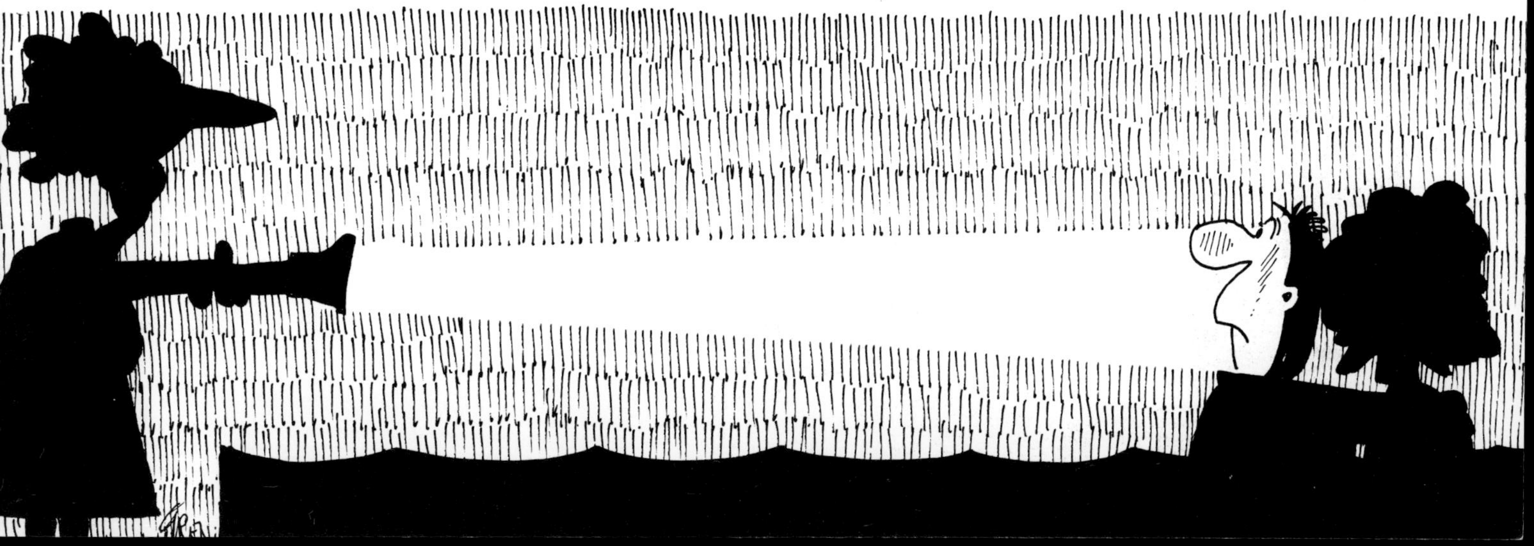

You're like shampoo upon my dandruff,
You're like glasses to my eyes;
And when you say I'm handsome
I just love your kindly lies.

You're my strength in all my efforts,
Without you I'd be nought;
You're my compass in direction
In doing what I ought.

You warm me like a cocktail,
You're my cherry on a stick;
You're bright and warm and glowing –
To my candle you're my wick.

You're the fruit that's in my punch bowl,
You're the twinkle in my dream.
You never let me down love,
To my hem you are my seam.

That alluring fragrance on the breeze
As the shade of memory slips,
That warming odour as we shared,
From a paper, all those chips.

You're the clip upon my filofax,
You're the crocus in my border;
Not only bringing colour, love,
You keep me well in order.

You're the trolley for my shopping,
You're the notes in my life's song;
I'm the grass box on your mower –
You carry me along.

The wind may blow, the rain may fall,
But I care not, not a jot.
To me it's always summer love
As our passion's always hot.

I love you more than anything,
To me you are much fairer
Than my hi-fi or my video
Or my Cosworth Ford Sierra.

Just like the breeze across my washing,
Just like strong drink when it's neat,
Just like the brush down our pathway
You sweep me off my feet.

You're the biscuit to my tea my love,
I'm your wrapping, you're my gift;
You're the jack beneath my car, my love,
You give me such a lift.

Love's path is sweet but rarely smooth –
That awful day you wept
Upon that hill, in your brand new clothes,
When you found in what you'd stepped.

You're the buckle on my sandal,
You're the biro on my cheque;
Like the stud that's on my collar
I love you hanging 'round my neck.

Like water 'bove my swimming trunks
You're the unexpected "Hey!";
Like double strength white peppermints
You take my breath away.

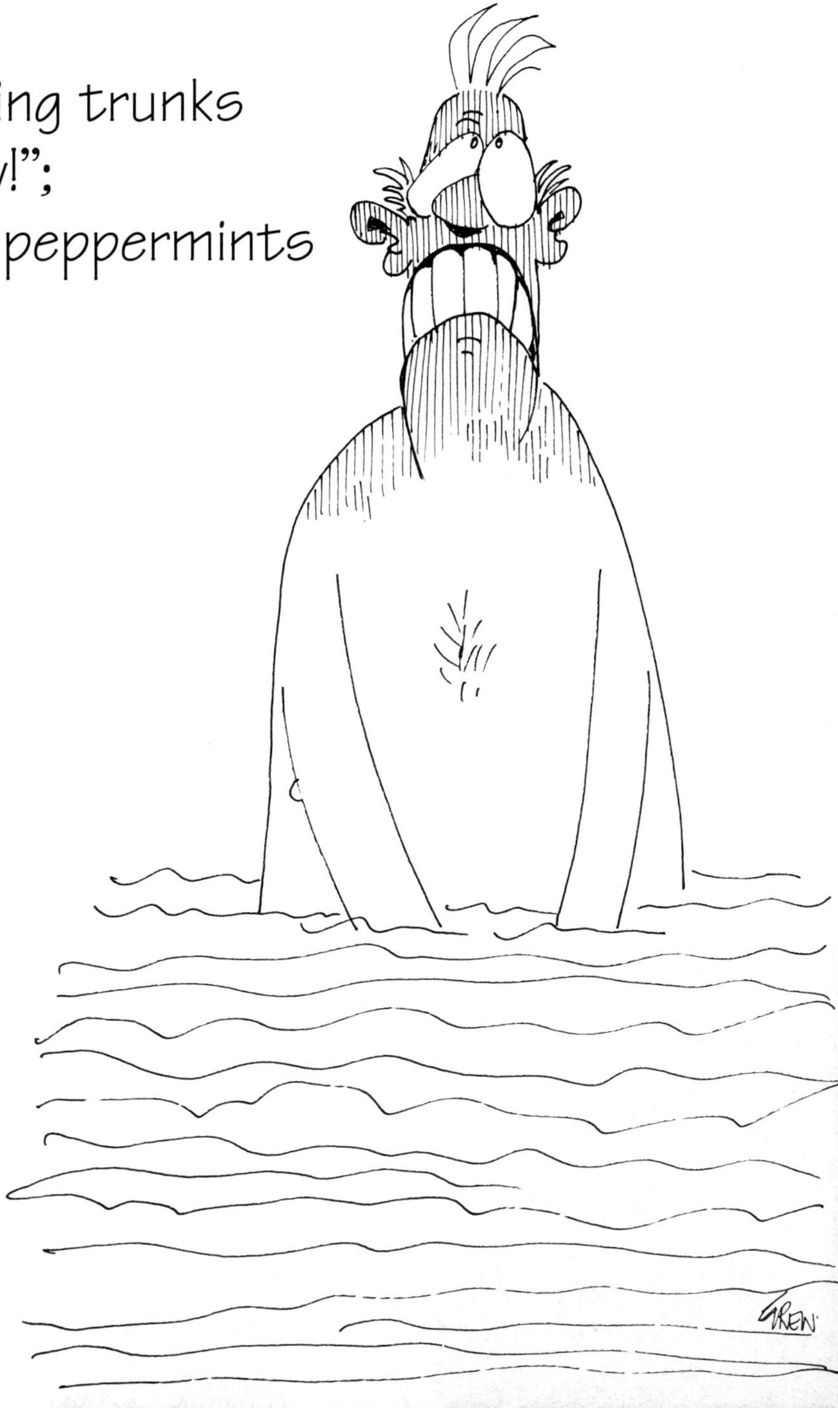

Like the shrubs are in our border,
Like the spring-cleaned glass is clear,
Our love is like a flower –
A perennial through the year.

Like the staple in my clipper,
Like the tin-tack on the wall,
Like a sticky tape on paper
We're together – through it all.

Like a fast ride in a funfair;
Like a nervous gasp, they say;
Like deodorant in my armpit
You take my breath away.

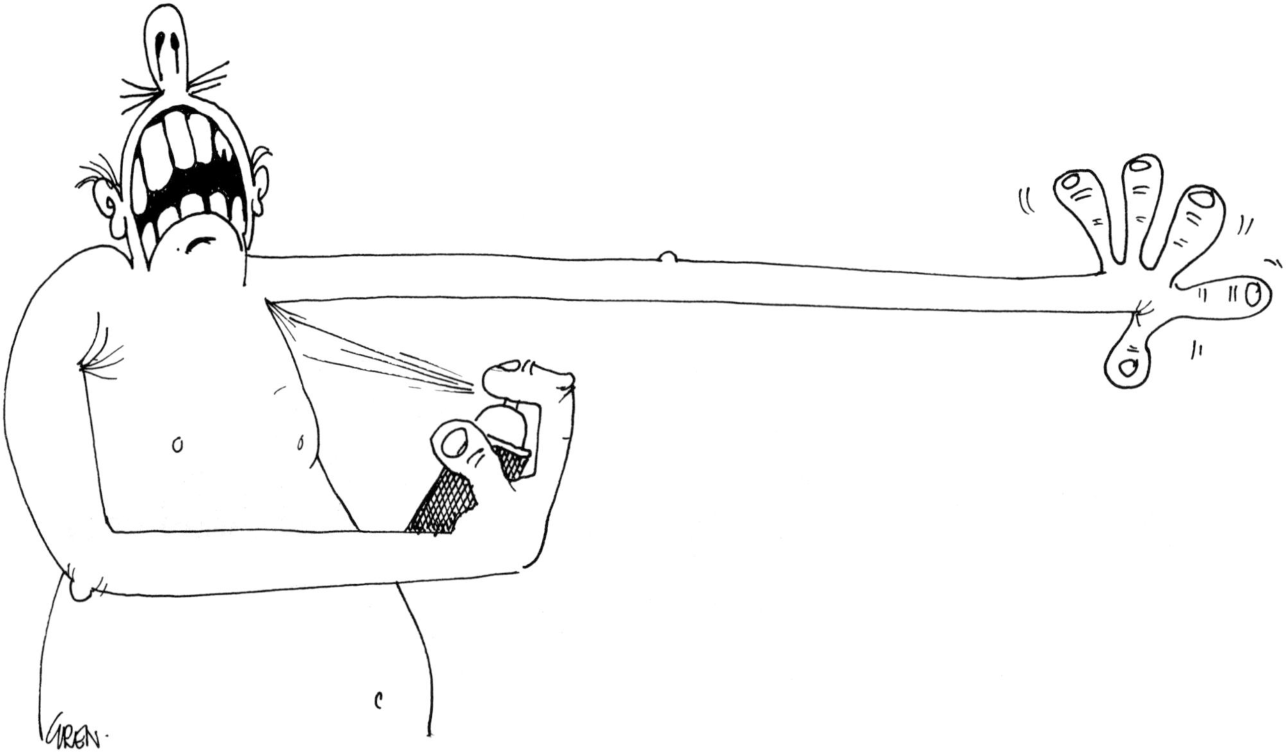

You make me feel much more a man,
You're supportive with no lapse.
You hold me close on life's each step,
You're like the laces in my daps.

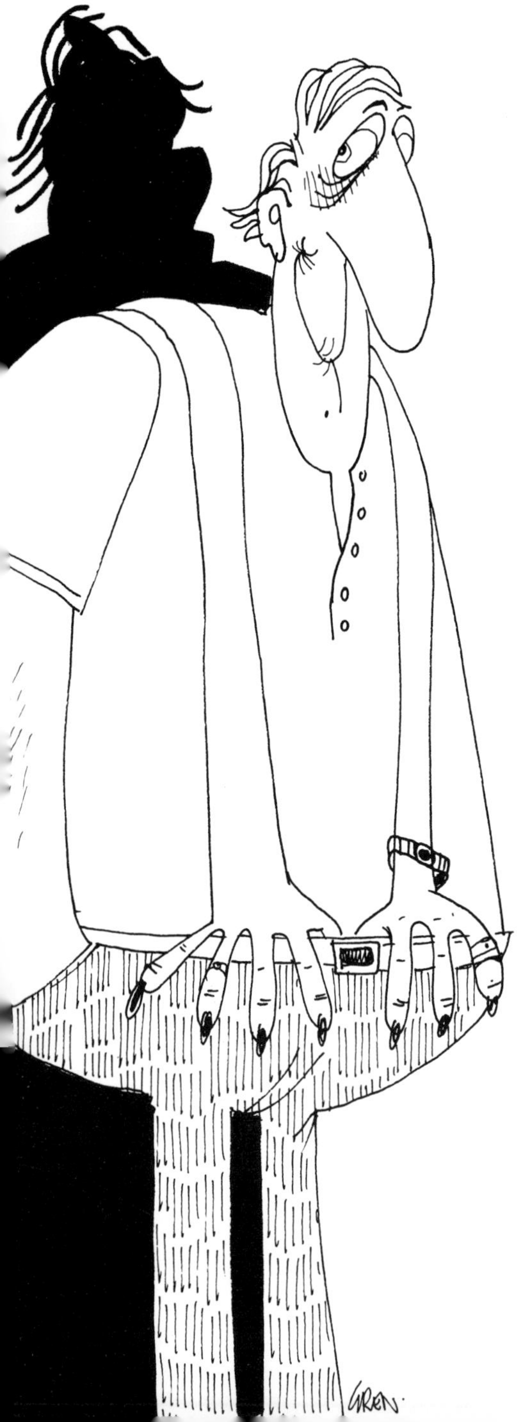

You're the wrapper round my parcel,
You're the belt around my slacks,
Your support so ever welcome
Like a rebate from the tax.

You lighten up my day for me –
You guide me like a map;
You're the sweetener in my cup of tea,
And the butter on my bap.

Your image comes at strange odd times,
It wafts its way to wend;
Like when I was beneath the car
And noticed its big end.

You're the flavour on my ice cream,
You're my cheese in fondue dips,
You're blancmange atop my jelly,
And vinegar on my chips.

You're the wine that flows in summer
Like fine nectar, only sweeter;
You're the motive in my thinking,
You're the shilling in my meter.

Your eyes throw stars of promise rare –
Their glint just leaves me shaken;
Your breath that blows upon me warm –
Was it beef or smokey bacon?

You're the cufflink in my shirt sleeve,
You're my cap in any weather,
You're our sellotape to us my love,
You hold us both together.

You're the black ones in my wine gum pack,
You're my zapper for life's telly,
You're that extra plus that makes life good
Like the lining in my welly.

It's little things I think of
When thoughts turn round to you;
You're natural – that's your secret –
With your 47 IQ.

I couldn't do without you,
You're my strength when life gets rough;
Outwardly so very smooth,
But like brillo, pretty tough.

That lovely night in winter time
We felt the chill air's whiff;
We stuck our ground – in rays of love –
Although quite frozen stiff.

You're the lights upon my Christmas tree –
A sparkly bauble looking good;
You're exciting, you're my cracker,
You're the sauce that's on my pud.

(and I want seconds!)

BBC RADIO WALES 882kHz MW

ARE YOU THE MUSING SORT OF ROMANTIC?

Do you have that licence to compose the same kind of poetic classics as Roy Noble?

If so, he would like to hear from you – and he may even air your compositions to the nation!

Send your verses to Roy at this address

Roy Noble Muses
BBC Radio Wales
Broadcasting House
Llandaff
Cardiff CF5 2YQ